WELCOME TO THE WORLD OF

Alligators
and Crocodiles

Diane Swanson

Whitecap Books

Edited by Elizabeth McLean
Cover design by Steve Penner
Interior design by Margaret Ng
Typeset by Jane Lightle
Photo research by Tanya Lloyd Kyi
Cover photograph by Stan Osolinski/Dembinsky Photo Assoc
Photo credits: Wayne Lynch iv, 2, 10; Lynn M. Stone 4, 20; Tony Rath/Naturalight Productions 6;
Rob and Ann Simpson 8; Dusty Perin/Dembinsky Photo Assoc 12;
Mark J. Thomas/Dembinsky Photo Assoc 14; Claudia Adams/Dembinsky Photo Assoc 16;
Jay Ireland & Georgienne Bradley 18, 26; Stan Osolinski/Dembinsky Photo Assoc 22, 24

The author thanks James Perran Ross, Crocodile Specialist Group, for his help.

Printed and bound in Hong Kong

For more information on this series and other Whitecap Books titles, visit our web site at www.whitecap.ca

National Library of Canada Cataloguing in Publication Data

Swanson, Diane, 1944–
  Welcome to the world of alligators and crocodiles

  Includes index.
  ISBN 1-55285-355-1

    1. Alligators—Juvenile literature. 2. Crocodiles—Juvenile literature. I. Title.
QL666.C925S92 2002   j597.98   C2002-910807-1

The publisher acknowledges the support of the Canada Council for the Arts and the Cultural Services Branch of the Government of British Columbia for our publishing program. We acknowledge the financial support of the Government of Canada through the Book Publishing Industry Development Program for our publishing activities.

Contents

World of Difference

THERE'S NOTHING PUNY ABOUT ALLIGATORS AND CROCODILES. They're the largest reptiles alive. A male American crocodile can easily stretch the length of a canoe and weigh more than three men. Its jaws are huge. Its tail is powerful. And its skin is thick and tough, like armor.

Not all crocodilians (CROK-uh-DILL-yuns)—a group of animals that includes both alligators and crocodiles—grow as big as American crocs. Still, the common caiman, North America's smallest crocodilian, can be as long as an average door.

Sometimes mistaken for a small crocodile, the common caiman is an alligator.

1

A smiling reptile? No, but the curvy jawline of an American crocodile looks like a grin.

Of the more than 20 kinds of crocodilians in the world, 4 live in North America, including Mexico. There are 2 gators— the American alligator and the common caiman—and 2 crocs—the American crocodile and the Morelet's crocodile.

You can tell alligators from crocodiles by checking their snouts. A gator's snout is usually wide and rounded, but a croc's is more slender and pointed. Look at the teeth, too. When a croc's mouth is shut, you'll spot a tooth close to the front of its bottom jaw, on each side. It pokes into a groove outside the top jaw. The same tooth on a gator is hidden when its mouth is closed.

Like other reptiles, such as lizards, snakes, and turtles, crocodilians are scale-covered animals that produce little heat. They lie in the sunshine to warm up.

GREAT GATORS, INCREDIBLE CROCS

Alligators and crocodiles often surprise people. Here are some of the reasons why:

- Alligators can pull their eyes into their skulls for protection.
- Crocs and gators swallow rocks, which may help them digest food and float flat out in the water.
- The jaws of an American alligator are strong enough to crunch an aluminum canoe.
- A crocodile that died in a zoo in 1997 was 115 years old!
- The nest of an American alligator can be a metre (3 feet) tall.

Where in the World

WETLANDS AND WARM WEATHER ATTRACT CROCODILIANS. They've made homes in parts of Africa, Asia, and Australia, as well as in North, Central, and South America.

American alligators, common caimans, and Morelet's crocodiles live mostly in and around fresh water in marshes, swamps, streams, lakes, and ponds. Sometimes they head into salty water for a short time.

American crocodiles live in both fresh and salty water. Now and then, storms sweep them right out to open seas. These crocodiles have special glands that help

The American alligator is right at home in a swamp.

A Morelet's crocodile slips into the stream to hunt.

remove the extra salt their body takes in.

When the weather is hot and dry, crocodilians may escape by digging burrows. They use their snouts, feet, and long strong tails to plow soft ground. American alligators might tunnel the length of a carport.

Gators also burrow to escape cold weather. In the southern United States, they may have to survive freezing temperatures. They seldom eat when it's cold. Instead, they draw on energy stored in their bodies.

American alligators can even live through wintry blasts by floating in the water. If ice at the surface freezes around the gators, they can't move. But as long as their nostrils are poking above the surface, they're able to breathe. Then the gators simply wait for a warm spell to set them free.

GATOR AID

Just doing what gators do, American alligators help other animals. In dry seasons, wetland birds, fish, snakes, turtles, and insects depend on water stored in holes made where gators wallow. In rainy seasons, gator-made paths worn in soft ground help drain off extra water.

Alligators feed on animals that devour a lot of plants, often saving wetlands from overgrazing. By eating dead creatures, gators act as cleanup teams, creating healthier homes for all.

World in Motion

ALL CROCODILIANS GET AROUND JUST FINE—on land and in water. But they're best suited for swimming. With their tails gently swishing, they cruise near the surface with barely more than their eyes and nostrils poking out. When they chase something—or when something chases them—the animals whip their mighty tails in S-shaped curves and zoom ahead.

If crocodilians want to sink out of sight, it's easy. They simply flick their feet upward, spread out their toes, and down they go. They can close their nostrils and ears, which keeps the water out.

It's the tail that powers a swimming crocodilian.

9

A common caiman
can travel a long
distance over land.

A crocodilian doesn't use its legs for swimming. It holds them close to its body. But the reptile can suddenly shoot out of the water and rush short distances on shore to snap at animals such as birds.

On land, a crocodilian often does the "high walk." It draws its legs nearly under itself, lifting its body well above the ground.

The high walk prevents the animal's undersides from scraping against rocks.

You can probably outrun a crocodilian, but don't even think about trying! From a standing start, it can reach full speed surprisingly fast.

If anything startles crocodilians, they usually head for water. They do the "belly crawl," sliding down over mud, or speed up to a "belly run." Pushing hard with their legs, they coast in curves and hit the water swimming.

Heading through a swamp, an American crocodile enters a snare. A cable of steel snaps tightly around its body. "Caught!" thinks the researcher as she slips a noose over the animal's snout. Then she tapes its jaws together.

Quickly, the researcher weighs, measures, and tags the croc. Then she removes the tape and frees the animal. For several days, she will follow it to see where it travels. She is learning that crocs need a lot of space.

World Full of Food

A turtle makes a
good meal for a
hungry alligator.

CROCODILIANS EAT WHATEVER CROCODILIANS CAN. Big ones often grab big prey, such as turtles, herons, and deer. They also gobble up little frogs, crabs, and insects, just as smaller kinds of crocodilians—and young ones—do.

Some kinds charge after particular foods. Mud turtles, for instance, are specials on menus for Morelet's crocodiles. But many crocodilians eat a lot of fish.

Resting in shallow water, a crocodilian waits to sense the movement of an approaching fish. Then, with a sudden snap of its jaws, it nabs the fish, pressing it against

Gone fishing! A crocodilian gets ready to down its catch.

a streambed or lake floor to get a solid grip. Next, the reptile pokes its head up above water and lets the fish drop down its throat. If the fish is especially large, the crocodilian might carry it ashore, holding or bashing it until it stops moving.

Surprise is what a crocodilian uses when it hunts. Blending in with floating plants, logs, and murky water, it swims slowly toward a wading bird. Or it lunges for a bigger animal that's drinking from shore and drags it underwater.

A crocodilian has more than twice as many teeth as you have, but it can't chew a thing. Small prey is gulped down whole. Large animals are torn into pieces. A crocodilian yanks and twists them until it rips off a chunk. In the process, the reptile might lose a few teeth, but that's no problem. Each tooth has a replacement, which soon moves into place.

TOSSING IT OUT

Owls do it. So do sharks. They cough up things they can't digest. It's a normal process—not a sign of sickness.

Healthy crocodiles also bring up stuff they can't use—like hairballs—but they're not able to vomit forcefully. Instead, they jerk their heads as if they're sneezing. Then they snap their jaws and shake their snouts from side to side. All that action helps release the waste that rises up their throats.

World of Words

AMERICAN ALLIGATORS ARE ESPECIALLY CHATTY, but all crocodilians "talk." They often make low-pitched sounds that travel well.

Alligators that go courting may "cough" or "purr" to their mates. The soft noises carry only a short distance. But gators can also bellow loudly, which seems to encourage other alligators to bellow as well.

If danger threatens, young crocodilians cry out, warning the others and calling adults for help. The grown animals— usually the parents—respond by threatening or attacking the enemy.

Close up, mating gators "speak" softly to each other.

Crocodile tears
are a good thing.
They help care
for the eyes.

Talking is nothing new for young crocodilians. They start grunting when they're still inside their eggs—particularly when they are ready to hatch. The grunts signal their parents to dig the eggs out of their deep nests.

Crocodilians use body language, such as headslapping, too. It's a way of announcing,

"We're here!" They lift their heads just above water, then open and close their big jaws fast. The movement creates a loud POP and a splash. Some crocodilians follow up by blowing bubbles, thrashing their tails, or roaring.

Headslaps grab the attention of other crocodilians in the neighborhood. They may rush to the surface of the water to copy the head-slap. The action helps bring many crocodilians together, especially during mating seasons.

CROCODILE TEARS

When people only pretend to feel sorry or sad, we say they're "crying crocodile tears." Alligators and crocodiles produce tears, but their "crying" says nothing about their feelings—either real or pretend.

Glands create moisture behind the animal's extra eyelids—the see-through lids that protect its eyes under-water. Tears smooth the movement of the lids, help clean the eyes, and probably fight bacteria, too.

19

New World

MOTHER CROCODILIANS LAY TOUGH, LEATHERY EGGS. Different kinds produce different numbers. American alligators produce about 45 eggs, while common caimans lay only half as many.

First, the female crocodilians build nests. They choose spots that won't likely get flooded by heavy rains and rising waters. American crocodiles usually dig holes and cover them with plants. Sometimes, these crocs just pile up plants and mud—as Morelet's crocodiles, common caimans, and American alligators normally do.

Like heaps of garden compost,

Fresh out of their eggs, crocodilians greet a new world.

21

A young alligator hitches a ride on mom's long tail.

crocodilian nests heat up as the plants inside them rot. That helps keep the eggs warm. For some crocodilians, the temperature of the eggs determines whether the hatchlings will be male or female. Warm eggs produce males; slightly cooler eggs produce females.

Crocodilian mothers often guard their nests for several weeks or months. They seldom leave—even to eat. The mothers protect the eggs from animals such as lizards.

Most crocodilians break through their shells, then wait for their mother to dig them out of the nest. She may help any unhatched young by lightly cracking their eggs in her mouth.

Mother crocodilians— and some fathers—may scoop up a group of hatchlings in their mouths. Then they give the young ones a safe ride to a nearby pond or stream.

Red-bellied turtles in Florida often lay eggs in American alligator nests. Gators guarding their eggs from egg-eaters such as raccoons just happen to protect turtle eggs, too. But these same gators eat some of the newly hatched turtles!

Still, more turtles may survive from eggs laid in alligator nests than from eggs laid elsewhere. If so, scientists wonder why. Does turtle survival depend on protection from egg-eaters, or flooding...or what?

Small World

The yellow bands on young American gators fade as the animals grow.

FOR SAFETY'S SAKE, CROCODILIANS STICK TOGETHER. During their first weeks or months, their mother stays with them, too. An American alligator mom often looks after her young for two or more years!

Groups of newly hatched crocodilians usually stay close to their nests, with their parents or other adults nearby. The mature crocodilians sometimes make sounds that tell the young ones, "Food is near."

At times, the sounds turn to warnings of danger: a hawk swooping low or a big fish swimming close. Adult crocodilians also defend the young by attacking enemies

The skull of an ancient crocodilian helps scientists learn how the animal has changed.

such as foxes. Still, in spite of all these efforts, only a few new members of any family live to be adults.

Young and old crocodilians depend on their senses to help them avoid trouble and find food. Their hearing is keen, and they smell very well. Above water, they have good sight—even in darkness. Their eyes have narrow, upright pupils that open wide at night, letting in more light than most round pupils do.

Throughout their lives, crocodilians keep growing. Young ones grow faster than old ones, especially where there's plenty of food and the weather stays warm all year. How long they survive partly depends on what kind of crocodilians they are. It's possible for American alligators to live more than 70 years, but common caimans might never be older than 40.

SUPERCROC!

As big as crocodiles get, they were once much bigger. In Africa's Sahara Desert, scientists uncovered a crocodile skull that's 110 million years old and as long as a tall man! They also pieced together half the animal's skeleton, which is twice the length of today's longest croc.

Nicknamed SuperCroc, the ancient creature might have weighed 8200 kilograms (18,000 pounds). It ate almost whatever its 130 teeth could grab—even dinosaurs!

Index